FOLENS
Ordnance Survey

UK ATLAS

Patricia Harrison

Steve Harrison

ACKNOWLEDGEMENTS

The authors and publishers would like to thank the following for permission to reproduce photographs and other materials:

Andy Bailey (28)
Birmingham National Exhibition Centre (34)
British Waterways (22)
Christine Moorcroft (16)
English Heritage (32)
Environmental Picture Library (23)
James Davis Travel Photography (8; 28; 38; 40)
JFP Galvin (18; 19)
Julie Smallwood (8)
Land Rover Public Affairs (34)
Lesley I Sampson (36)
Life File Photographic Library (10; 11; 13; 15; 30)
Malcolm Watson (40)
North West Waterboard (15)
Northern Ireland Tourist Board (42)
Oliver-Murphy / Metro Centre (32)
Ronald Sheridan's Photo Library, Ancient Art and Architecture Collection (22; 36)
Science Photo Library (cover, 1; 13)
Select Photo Agency and Picture Library (13; 17; 20; 34; 38; 40)
Shorts Brothers plc (42)
The Pepsi Max Big One by Lord Lichfield at Blackpool Pleasure Beach (30)
the Still Moving *picture company* (24; 26)
Tom Mackie (36)
Topham Picturepoint (19; 23; 28; 42)
WorldSat International Inc. (4; 5)
York & County Press (16; 17; 18)

The publishers have made every effort to contact copyright holders but this has not always been possible. If any have been overlooked we will be pleased to make any necessary arrangements.

To the best of the publishers' knowledge, information in this atlas was correct at the time of going to press. No responsibility can be accepted for any errors.

On pages 12, 14, 15, 16, 17, 18 and 19 of this atlas, mapping of Ireland is based on the Ordnance Survey with the permission of:
1) The Government of the Republic of Ireland (Permit No 6002)
2) The Controller of HM Stationary Office (Permit No 752)
Crown copyright reserved.

Graphics and design: Alan Kennedy of Ordnance Survey Design Services, Steve Jaycock of Design For Marketing.
Artwork: Stephen Abbot of Ordnance Survey Design Services, Steve Jaycock.
Cover design: John Hawkins of Design For Marketing.
Edited by: Edward Rippeth

First published 1995 by Folens Limited, Dunstable and Dublin, and Ordnance Survey, Southampton.

© 1995 Folens Limited, on behalf of the authors. Revised Edition 1998.
© Crown Copyright 1995.

	non-net	**net**
ISBN	1 852 76841 X (Folens)	
ISBN	0 319 00588 7 (OS)	0 319 00774 X (OS)

Printed in Singapore by Craft Print.

CONTENTS

EUROPE from Space

Weather satellites circle the earth at a height of about 820km and send back hundreds of images. These are pieced together to form a large image without clouds. Shading is added to make the height of the land clearer.

The Atlantic Ocean lies between Europe and America. It is probably named after Atlantis, a large island from Greek legend, which was believed to have been destroyed by an earthquake. At its deepest point the Atlantic is 8648m deep. This is almost as deep as Mount Everest is high!

The Strait of Gibraltar is only 13km across. It separates Africa and Europe, and the Mediterranean Sea from the Atlantic Ocean. In ancient legend the two large rocks north and south of the strait were once joined. Hercules was said to have parted them. That is why they were once known as the pillars of Hercules. Today we call them the Rock of Gibraltar and Jebel Musa.

The Mediterranean Sea is between Europe to the north and Africa to the south and Asia to the east. Mediterranean means centre of the Earth! In the past, Europeans knew nothing of America or Australia. They thought all the world's land surrounded the Mediterranean.

The seas in the far north freeze over in winter. The Norwegian Sea and the Barents Sea are both part of the Arctic Ocean.

Lake Ladoga is Europe's largest lake. It is joined to the Gulf of Finland by the River Neva.

The Ural Mountains mark the Eastern edge of Europe. Beyond them lies Asia. They stretch from the Arctic Circle in the north to the Caspian Sea.

The Volga is Europe's largest river. It is 3531km long.

The Caspian Sea is the largest inland sea in the world. Its western shore is in Europe. It has no tide. Its deepest point is about 1000m deep.

The Caucasus Mountains stand between Europe and Asia. They stretch west-east between the Black Sea. The highest peak is Mount Elbrus which is 5642m high.

The Bosporus is the stretch of water which links the Mediterranean Sea and the Black Sea. It also separates Europe and Asia. The Bosporus is 27km long and is only 600m across at its narrowest point.

EUROPE Political

Population

The total population of Europe is about 720 million. One in seven of the world's population lives in Europe.

Cities with over 2 million people

Moscow 9 million

1 million people

Paris 8.75 million

Istanbul 4 million

London 7 million

Berlin 3.3 million

St Petersburg 5 million

Madrid 3.1 million

Athens 3 m

Kiev 2.5 m

Rome 2.8 m

Budapest 2.1 m

Note: Istanbul has parts in both Asia and Europe

Living in Town and Country

The population of a country can be divided into those who live in towns (urban population) and those who live in the countryside (rural population). The percentage of people in rural areas is falling steadily.

94% UK	97% Belgium
75% France	35% Portugal

Urban   Rural

Population density is the number of people living in a square area of land 1km long and 1km wide (a square kilometre). To work out the population density of a country we divide the population by area of land in square kilometres.

$$\frac{\text{Population}}{\text{Area of land}} = \text{Population density}$$

The population density for the whole of Europe is 96 people per sq km. Only Asia has a higher density.

Netherlands 366   Iceland 2

People per sq km

Country	People	Country	People
Netherlands	366	Spain	78
Belgium	323	Ireland	53
UK	234	Sweden	19
Germany	218	Finland	15
Italy	189	Norway	13
France	102	Iceland	2

Travel

In the past, travel to the capitals of Europe was often slow, uncomfortable and expensive. Today more and more people visit capital cities for weekend breaks or business. London's airports have the best international connections in the world. The new Channel Tunnel provides a direct rail link to European capitals.

Distances from London

Athens 2400 km

Moscow 2500 km

Berlin 950 km

Reykjavik 1850 km

Helsinki 1850 km

Amsterdam 400 km

Lisbon 1550 km

Budapest 1500 km

EUROPE Political

The countries of Turkey and Russia are partly in Europe and partly in Asia. Only European parts are shown here in colour.

ASIA

AFRICA

Key
★ Capital city
— Country boundary

One millimetre on this map is the same as 35 kilometres on the ground.

0   10   20   30

NORTH ATLANTIC OCEAN

Norwegian Sea

Barents Sea

Arctic Circle

ICELAND
★ Reykjavik

RUSSIA

Pechora
Vychegda
Sev. Dvina
Kama
Ural
Sukhona
Volga
White Sea
Lake Onega
Lake Ladoga
Moscow ★
St Petersburg ●
Volga
Don
Caspian Sea

FINLAND
★ Helsinki
Gulf of Bothnia

SWEDEN
★ Stockholm

NORWAY
★ Oslo

Baltic Sea
Copenhagen ★
DENMARK

North Sea

ESTONIA
Riga
LATVIA
LITHUANIA Vilnius
RUSSIA

Minsk ★
BELARUS

Kiev ★
UKRAINE
Dnieper
Chişinău ★
MOLDOVA
Sea of Azov
Black Sea
Bucharest ★
ROMANIA
Danube
BULGARIA Sofia ★
Istanbul ●
TURKEY
MACEDONIA Skopje ★
Tirana ★
ALBANIA
GREECE
Athens ★
Aegean Sea
Ionian Sea

POLAND
★ Warsaw
Oder

Berlin ★
GERMANY
Elbe

NETHER- LANDS
Amsterdam ★
Brussels ★
BELGIUM
LUXEMBOURG

Prague ★
CZECH REPUBLIC
SLOVAKIA Bratislava ★
Vienna ★
AUSTRIA
LIECHTENSTEIN
SLOVENIA
Ljubljana ★
Zagreb ★
CROATIA
BOSNIA HERZEGOVINA
Sarajevo ★
Belgrade ★
YUGOSLAVIA
Adriatic Sea

SWITZERLAND
Bern ★

FRANCE
Paris ★
Seine
Loire
Garonne
Rhône

ITALY
Rome ★
SAN MARINO
Mediterranean Sea

Bay of Biscay

UNITED KINGDOM
REPUBLIC OF IRELAND
Dublin ★
Celtic Sea

SPAIN
Madrid ★
ANDORRA
Ebro
Tagus
PORTUGAL
Lisbon ★

N
E
S
W

60° N
45° N
45° N
30° N

15° W
0°
15° E
30° E
45° E

A   B   C   D

EUROPE Physical

The physical world is always changing, but it is a very slow change. At different times in the distant past, parts of Europe have been covered by deserts, by warm seas and by ice. Europe is still changing.

New land can appear. In the last few years, volcanic activity around Iceland has created new islands. The steam from this geyser is evidence of the active heat beneath the surface.

The fjords of Norway were formed by ice sheets (glaciers) which carved through the rock forming deep valleys. When the climate warmed and the ice melted the sea flowed into these valleys.

Glaciers are still active in Europe today. As they move they scrape great boulders from mountain sides and loosen the rock below them.

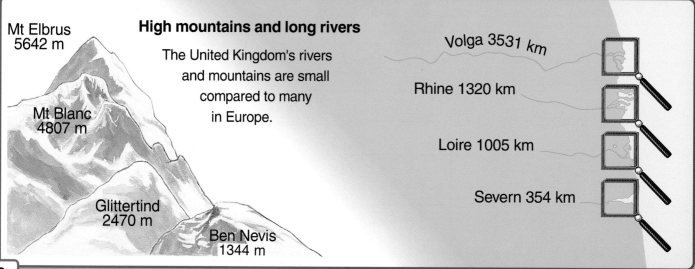

High mountains and long rivers

The United Kingdom's rivers and mountains are small compared to many in Europe.

Mt Elbrus 5642 m

Mt Blanc 4807 m

Glittertind 2470 m

Ben Nevis 1344 m

Volga 3531 km

Rhine 1320 km

Loire 1005 km

Severn 354 km

EUROPE
Physical

Height in metres

- Over 2000
- 1000 – 2000
- 200 – 1000
- 0 – 200
- Below sea level

Key
- Rivers
- Lakes

One millimetre on this map is the same as 35 kilometres on the ground.

0   10   20   30

Barents Sea

Ural Mountains

Pechora
Vychegda
Kama
Ural
Sev-Dvina
Sukhona
Volga
Volga
Don
Caspian Sea
Mount Elbrus
Caucasus Mts
Sea of Azov
Black Sea
Bosporus
Dnieper
Dnester
Danube
Carpathians
Aegean Sea
Ionian Sea
Adriatic Sea
Mediterranean Sea

White Sea
Lake Onega
Lake Ladoga
Neva
Daugava
Oder
Elbe
Rhine
Po
Alps
Mont Blanc
Rhone
Pyrenees
Ebro
Tagus
Strait of Gibraltar

Gulf of Bothnia
Ume älv
Baltic Sea
Lake Vänern
Lake Vättern
Kjölen Mountains
Glittertind
North Sea
Thames
Seine
Loire
Garonne
Bay of Biscay
Ben Nevis
Celtic Sea

Norwegian Sea

Arctic Circle

NORTH
ATLANTIC
OCEAN

N
E
S
W

60° N
45° N
45° N
30° E
15° E
0°
15° W
30° N
45° N

9

EUROPE in winter

ASIA

ASIA

ASIA

AFRICA

Athens

40 30 20 10 0 -10 -20 °C	250 200 150 100 50 0 mm

Temperature Range 20°C

Rainfall Total 402 mm

J F M A M J J A S O N D

Moscow

40 30 20 10 0 -10 -20 °C	250 200 150 100 50 0 mm

Temperature Range 32°C

Rainfall Total 624 mm

J F M A M J J A S O N D

London

40 30 20 10 0 -10 -20 °C	250 200 150 100 50 0 mm

Temperature Range 16°C

Rainfall Total 593 mm

J F M A M J J A S O N D

Average rainfall and temperatures in Europe

The Alps. High mountains and bright sunshine mean good skiing conditions.

Northern Finland. In northern Europe the winter sun shines for only a few hours each day.

Seas and places

Barents Sea

White Sea

• Archangel

☆ Moscow

Sea of Azov

Black Sea

Gulf of Bothnia

Baltic Sea

Aegean Sea

☆ Athens

Ionian Sea

Adriatic Sea

Palermo •

Mediterranean Sea

Norwegian Sea

North Sea

London ☆

Bay of Biscay

Madrid ☆

Celtic Sea

NORTH ATLANTIC OCEAN

Key

Temperature °C

- Over 10
- 5–10
- 0–5
- 0–-5
- -5–-10
- Below -10

☆ Capital city

• Other city or town

One millimetre on this map is the same as 45 kilometres on the ground.

0 10 20 30

EUROPE in summer

Average rainfall and temperatures in Europe

Europe has many popular holiday destinations. Some people visit the hot, sunny coastal destinations of the Mediterranean. Other people prefer the clear air and scenery of the mountains.

Map labels

Barents Sea

White Sea

Archangel •

Moscow ⊛

Caspian Sea

Sea of Azov

Black Sea

Aegean Sea

Athens ⊛

Ionian Sea

Mediterranean Sea

Adriatic Sea

Palermo

Gulf of Bothnia

Baltic Sea

Norwegian Sea

North Sea

London ⊛

Bay of Biscay

Celtic Sea

Madrid ⊛

NORTH ATLANTIC OCEAN

Climate graphs

Graph 1 (top)
Temperature Range 14°C
Rainfall Total 512 mm
J F M A M J J A S O N D

Graph 2 (middle)
Temperature Range 22°C
Rainfall Total 444 mm
J F M A M J J A S O N D

Graph 3 (bottom)
Temperature Range 31°C
Rainfall Total 530 mm
J F M A M J J A S O N D

Scale °C: 40 30 20 10 0 -10 -20 °C
Rainfall mm: 250 200 150 100 50 0 mm

Key

Temperature °C

- Over 25
- 20–25
- 15–20
- 10–15
- 5–10
- 0–5

⊛ Capital city
• Other city or town

One millimetre on this map is the same as 45 kilometres on the ground.

Scale: 0 10 20 30

UNITED KINGDOM Political

The Union Flag

Scotland

England

1606 First Union Flag

Saltire of St Patrick

Union Flag since 1801

NORTHERN IRELAND

Ireland was divided into separate kingdoms in the Middle Ages. Henry II of England invaded and became Lord of Ireland in 1175. There were many outbreaks of fighting against the English rulers. Settlers were sent from England and Scotland, especially to north eastern Ireland (Ulster). In 1801 the whole of Ireland was joined to Great Britain and a new name, the United Kingdom, was used. The cross of St Patrick (shown above) was added to the existing British flag to make the Union Flag flown today. Many Irish people fought against this union. In 1921 Ireland was divided, and the south became the Irish Free State (later Eire). Most of Ulster remained in the United Kingdom to become Northern Ireland.

SCOTLAND

In 1603 King James VI of Scotland also became King James I of England. To show that he ruled one country James called his new kingdom Great Britain, meaning large Britain, but it was not until 1707 that the two countries were united.

WALES

In 1301, King Edward I of England conquered Wales and declared his son Prince of Wales. Wales was officially joined with England in 1543.

ENGLAND

In Anglo-Saxon times England was divided into seven kingdoms. By 1066 it was a single kingdom.

⊛ Capital city
• Other city or town
— Country boundary

One millimetre on this map is the same as 5 kilometres on the ground.

0   10   20   30

Shetland Islands
Lerwick

Orkney Islands

Outer Hebrides

Stornoway

SCOTLAND

Inverness

Aberdeen

Dundee
Perth

Glasgow
Edinburgh ⊛

Ayr

ATLANTIC OCEAN

Derry / Londonderry

NORTHERN IRELAND
⊛ Belfast

IRELAND

Isle of Man
⊛ Douglas

Irish Sea

Blackpool

Liverpool

Holyhead
Anglesey
Bangor
Wrexham

St George's Channel

Aberystwyth

WALES

Newport

Swansea

Cardiff ⊛

Celtic Sea

Newcastle upon Tyne
Sunderland
Carlisle
Middlesbrough

North Sea

Kingston upon Hull
Bradford   Leeds
Manchester
Sheffield

Nottingham

Wolverhampton Birmingham
Coventry

Peterborough

Norwich

Ipswich

ENGLAND

Luton

London ⊛

Bristol

Southampton
Portsmouth   Brighton

Exeter

Isle of Wight

Plymouth

Isles of Scilly

English Channel

Channel Islands

N
W   E
S

This satellite image is not what you could actually see from space. The satellite has taken many photos of the United Kingdom and a computer has turned these into a single image we can understand. The Earth is curved, so the computer adjusts the images to produce a flat picture. This image helps show population density.

UNITED KINGDOM
Population

The density of population is the number of people living in one square kilometre of land. Different parts of the UK have different population densities.

In northern Scotland there are fewer than 25 people for every square kilometre. In parts of London 10 000 people live in a square kilometre.

Key

- Pasture
- Arable Land
- Urban Areas
- Coastal Sand
- Mixed Moorland & Forest

One millimetre on this map is the same as 5 kilometres on the ground.

| 0 | 10 | 20 | 30 |

More than nine out of ten people live in towns and cities in the UK. This is one of the highest figures in the world.

Fewer than two people out of 100 work in farming in the UK. This is one of the lowest figures in the world.

UNITED KINGDOM
Physical

There is a link between the height of land and weather conditions. Our changing weather comes mainly from the west. Winds blowing from the Atlantic carry rain to the United Kingdom.

The high land in the west forces the rain clouds to rise. As they do so they cool and drop their rain. Look at the rainfall map on page 15 and compare the areas of heaviest rainfall with the physical map on this page.

Height in metres

- Over 1000
- 500 – 1000
- 200 – 500
- 100 – 200
- 0 – 100

Depth in metres

- 0 – 100
- 100 – 200
- 200 – 1000
- Over 1000

Key

- ~~~~ Rivers
- Lakes
- ▲ Spot heights

One millimetre on this map is the same as 5 kilometres on the ground.

0   10   20   3(

Northwest Highlands

Moray Firth

Loch Ness

Great Glen

Spey

Grampian Mountains

Dee

Ben Nevis 1344m ▲

Tay

Loch Lomond

Forth

Firth of Forth

Clyde

North Sea

Firth of Clyde

Southern Uplands

Tweed

Nith

Cheviot Hills

Tyne

Wear

Tees

Solway Firth

Cumbrian Mountains

Scafell Pike 977m ▲

Lake Windermere

Pennines

North York Moors

Ouse

Humber

Foyle

Sperrin Mts

Mourne

Antrim Mts

Lough Neagh

Belfast Lough

Slieve Donard 852m

Mourne Mts ▲

Dundalk Bay

Morecambe Bay

Mersey

The Wash

Trent

Norfolk Broads

Irish Sea

Snowdon 1085m ▲

Conwy

Caernarfon Bay

Llyn Trawsfynydd

Llyn Tegid

Cambrian Mountains

Severn

Avon

Cotswold Hills

Great Ouse

Chiltern Hills

Cardigan Bay

Teifi

Usk

Brecon Beacons

Avon

Mendip Hills

Thames

North Downs

ATLANTIC OCEAN

Celtic Sea

St George's Channel

Bristol Channel

Exmoor

Exe

South Downs

The Solent

Dartmoor

Tamar

Land's End

English Channel

Ben Nevis 1344m

Snowdon 1085m

Scafell Pike 977m

Slieve Donard 852m

Highest mountains in each country

The satellite image on page 13 shows that most large cities are on low land, away from high mountains.

elief rainfall

Heat of sun

Wind

Clouds cool, rain falls

Rain shadow; little rain Dry as clouds descend and air warms

Evaporation

River

is rainfall map shows that most n falls on the mountains, pecially in the far west where v people live.

Rainfall is low in the South East and eastern England. Droughts are common. This is made worse as the need for water is growing as people move to the area to find work.

Rainfall (mm)

More than 1800

1200 – 1800

800 – 1200

600 – 800

0 – 600

In 1894 Manchester City Corporation had a 96 mile (154 km) aqueduct built from Thirlmere, a lake in the Lake District, to Manchester to provide water for the people and for industry.

GEOLOGY

Geology is the study of the Earth beneath our feet. This map shows the main types of rock found in the United Kingdom.

The rock type can influence industry. Many homes in Britain have slate roofs made from the finest Welsh slate.

In parts of eastern England the sea easily erodes the clay cliffs. Cliff-top houses are destroyed each year.

Different rock types provide suitable locations for different plants. For example, Bloody Cranesbill grows on limeston wild thyme thrives on chalk.

One millimetre on this map is the same as 6 kilometres on the ground.

0   10   20   30

Water can dissolve limestone to form underground caves.

Key

Sedimentary: Formed from tiny water creatures, plants, sand and mud that s: to the bed of rivers or the sea and were squeezed toget Limestone, chalk, sandstone and mudstone are all sediment

Chalk — A white fine-grained limestone made of tiny sea creatur

Limestone — Carboniferous limestone is hard and grey. It is made of shelled creatures.

Igneous: Deep below the Earth's surface are rocks so hot that they are liq (magma).

Volcanic — Igneous rock which has cooled at or near the Earth's surfa (for example, basalt).

Intrusive — Igneous rock which cooled more slowly below the Earth's surfa (for example, granite).

Metamorphic: Rocks that have changed by being heated or squeezed (for example, slate and marble).

RIVERS AND LAKES

...ivers were once main routes for travelling
...cross the country. The Vikings sailed their
...hips up the rivers to raid and later to settle.
...ondon was once the world's busiest port.
...hips sailed up the Thames to the many
...ondon docks.

Key
Rivers
Lakes

ATLANTIC
OCEAN

**Map labels:**

Naver · Thurso · Moray Firth · Loch Ness · Spey · Dee · Tay · Earn · Loch Lomond · Forth · Firth of Forth · Clyde · Firth of Clyde · Ayr · Nith · Annan · Tweed · Teviot · Tyne · Wear · Tees · Eden · Derwent · Solway Firth · Foyle · Bann · Mourne · Main · Belfast Lough · Lough Neagh · Lower Lough Erne · Blackwater · Bann · Strangford Lough · Upper Lough Erne · Lake District · Lune · Derwent · Ribble · Aire · Ouse · Morecambe Bay · Mersey · Don · Humber · Caernarfon Bay · Dee · Trent · Witham · Bain · The Wash · Slea · Wensum · Bure · Yare · Norfolk Broads · Cardigan Bay · Welland · Nene · Waveney · Severn · Great Ouse · Stour · Colne · Teifi · Blackwater · Tywi · Usk · Thames · Avon · Medway · Bristol Channel · Avon · Test · Frome · The Solent · Exe · Strait of Dover · Tamar · Fal · English Channel · Irish Sea · North Sea

Replica Viking ships on the
River Ouse at York.

DANGER
THAMES WATER IS POLLUTED WATER
BEWARE WEIL'S DISEASE
BEWARE BACTERIA
BEWARE ILLEGAL DISCHARGE
DO NOT SWIM HERE

N W E S

...any rivers are badly polluted.
...id rain and the discharge
...chemicals from industry can
...llute rivers and lakes, killing
...h and other river life. Strict
...ntrols have meant many
...ers have become cleaner
...er the past few years.

One millimetre on this
map is the same as 5
kilometres on the
ground.

0   10   20   30

Many settlements were
formed and then grew
beside rivers, often at a
crossing point.

WINTER WEATHER in the UK

In winter the west of Britain is warmer than inland and the east. The sea has a warming effect on the land, raising temperatures near the coast. Towns are warmer than country areas.

Temperature (°C)
Average January temperature

- More than 7°
- 6–7°
- 5–6°
- 4–5°
- 3–4°
- Less than 3°

More snow falls on higher ground than on lower ground. There is more snow in the north than the south. Snow forms in clouds which are at freezing temperatures and below.

Snow laying
Average number of mornings with lying snow

- 0–10
- 11–20
- 21–50
- Over 50

Fog is tiny droplets of water in the air. On a night without cloud the earth loses heat rapidly. The air above the ground also cools. Moisture in the air turns to droplets, especially tehwere there is pollution. When there is no wind the fog can last all day.

...he south of Britain is much warmer than the ...orth. The coast is cooler than inland because ...e sea has a cooling effect on the land.

...ost lightning occurs in summer. An electric ...arge builds up in a cloud and this is ...scharged to another cloud or to the ground. ...his lightning spark heats the air causing an ...plosion, which we hear as thunder. Eastern ...ngland has the most thunderstorms.

Temperature (˚C)
Average July temperatures.

▓	More than 17˚
▒	16˚–17˚
▒	15˚–16˚
░	14˚–15˚
░	13˚–14˚
░	Less than 13˚

...unshine
...verage daily duration ...bright sunshine, ...hours.

	More than 5.0
	4.5–5.0
	4.0–4.5
	3.5–4.0
	3.0–3.5
	Less than 3.0

The long daylight hours of summer mean most sunshine occurs in June. The least sunshine is in December. The cloudier and wetter areas have least sunshine.

Cumulus clouds form when the sun heats the ground. The air above the ground warms and rises. As it rises it cools and water vapour changes to tiny droplets. Power stations can also produce cumulus clouds.

COMMUNICATIONS

More and more people own cars and use them for travel to work. Many motorways in the United Kingdom are jammed with traffic, made worse by road repairs.

One solution is to increase the number of people using public transport. However, that means more fast, reliable buses and trains at a price that people can afford.

Key

M5	Motorways
A19	Important A-Roads
•	Towns

One millimetre on this map is the same as 5 kilometres on the ground.

0   10   20

Shetland Islands

Orkney Islands

Isle of Lewis

Thurso
A882
A9
Helmsdale
Ullapool
Dornoch
A835
Fraserburgh
A96 A9
A98
Peterhead
Inverness
A96
Kyle of Lochalsh
A9
Grantown-on-Spey
Isle of Skye
A87
Kingussie
Aberdeen
Mallaig
A96
A93
A830
Fort William
A9
Forfar
A90
Montrose
A82
Pitlochry
Oban
A85
A88
Perth
Dundee
Inveraray
St Andrews
A816
A84
A91
Stirling
A82
A90
EDINBURGH
North Sea
A83
Glasgow
M8
A68
Berwick-upon-Tweed
A78 A77 M74
M73
Peebles
A1
Campbeltown
Ayr
A72
Lanark
A76
Moffat
A68
A696
Newcastle upon Tyne
Girvan
A77
A74(M)
Dumfries
A69
Londonderry
A2
Stranraer
A75
A596
Carlisle
A1(M)
A5
A2
A26 A36
Larne
Workington
A66
Penrith
A19
Omagh
A505
M2
M1
BELFAST
A595
A590
Darlington
A171
Scarborough
A82
A5
Armagh
A24
Isle of Man
A65
A1
A65
A685
A4

Irish Sea

Blackpool
M55
M65
Leeds
A63
Kingston upon Hull
York
MANCHESTER
M62
M180
Doncaster
Liverpool
A628
A16
A1
Sheffield
Holyhead
A5
M56
A61 A60
A17
Cromer
A148
Caernarfon
A55
A52 M1
Boston
A140
Chester
A41
Nottingham
A16
A52
M6
A46
Norwich
A470 A494 A483
Shrewsbury
A5
Leicester
A47
A487
A458
A43 A1
A10
A12
Lowestoft
Dolgellau
A442
M54
A14
Ipswich
Cardigan Bay
BIRMINGHAM
A45
M69
Northampton
Cambridge
Aberystwyth
A44
Llangurig
M42
A6
A14
A487
M5 M40 A43
M1
A41
Colchester
A470
A49
Gloucester
A1(M)
M25
Chelmsford
Fishguard
A465
Monmouth
Oxford
M40
A40
Carmarthen
A48
A40
Swindon
LONDON
A40
Newbury
M4
A2
Swansea
CARDIFF
M4
Bristol
M3
Dover
Bath
Salisbury
Winchester
M25 M23
Folkestone
A361
Taunton
A30
M27
A23 A259
Brighton
Bude
A39
Southampton
Portsmouth
Eastbourne
Exeter
A35
A31
A30
Bournemouth
Dorchester
Land's End
Plymouth
Penzance
A38
A30

ATLANTIC OCEAN

St George's Channel

Celtic Sea

Bristol Channel

English Channel

N
W   E
S

20

The development of the railways

The world's first steam railways were in the United Kingdom. The Stockton–Darlington railway opened in 1825. The first intercity railway joined Manchester to Liverpool in 1830.

1851

By 1851 most large towns were linked by railways.

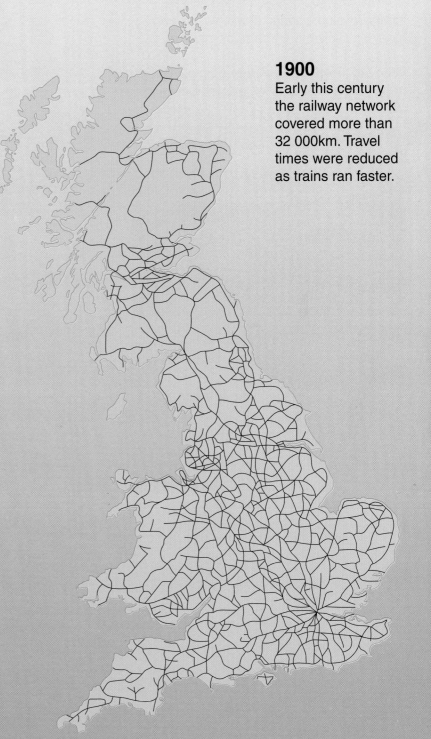

1900
Early this century the railway network covered more than 32 000km. Travel times were reduced as trains ran faster.

1997

In the 1930s road building began to increase. Other forms of transport began to replace the train. In the 1960s many railway lines and small stations were closed.

TRANSPORT

The Romans constructed roads throughout Britain, so that the army could be moved quickly wherever it was needed and trade could develop. London, the main city and port, was linked to all parts by major roads.

Many of these roads were kept in good repair even after the Romans left Britain in AD409.

Major roads in Roman Britain

Key
— Roman Road
– – – Roman Wall
● Roman Town
EBVRACVM
(York)

Inchtuthil
Inveresk
ANTONNINE WALL
HADRIAN'S WALL
LVGVVALIVM (Carlisle)
ARBEIA (South Shields)
BREMETENACVM VETERANORVM (Ribchester)
EBVRACVM (York)
PETVARIA (Brough)
LINDVM (Lincoln)
DEVA (Chester)
VIROCONIVM (Wroxeter)
RATAE (Leicester)
VENTA (Caistor St Edmund)
GLEVVM (Gloucester)
CORINIVM (Cirencester)
CAMVLODVNVM (Colchester)
ISCA (Caerleon)
VERVLAMIVM (St Albans)
RVTVPIAE (Richborough)
AQVAE SVLIS (Bath)
CALLEVA (Silchester)
LONDINIVM (London)
PORTVS DVBRIS (Dover)
ISCA (Exeter)
DVRNOVARIA (Dorchester)
NOVIOMAGVS (Chichester)
FOSSE WAY
WATLING STREET
ERMINE STREET

The canal age 1760–1840

Road communications were poor for many centuries. In the eighteenth century much of Britain's trade travelled by sea around the coast rather than across country.

In the 1760s canal building began. Cities were linked for trade and transport was better and cheaper. The railways (see page 21) took much of the canal trade in the next century. Today the canal and river system of Great Britain covers 3,200 km of water. Three-quarters of it is used for leisure boating and fishing.

In 1958 the first stretch of motorway in Britain was opened. It was called the Preston bypass and is now part of the M6. In 1959 a large part of the M1 was opened. Unlike earlier main roads, motorways are designed to avoid town centres and reduce journey times.

Motorways in 1964

Today there is disagreement about motorways. They are supposed to speed up journeys, but some people think they just encourage more cars on the road. Motorways are being widened and repaired. Since 1985 some motorways have been widened to eight lanes or more. Even so traffic jams have grown worse, wasting time and money.

Today's motorways

SCOTLAND

The north and west of Scotland has high mountains, magnificent scenery, high rainfall and few people. Most of the population lives in lowland Scotland. Oil and gas discoveries in the North Sea have brought jobs and money to the north-east of Scotland. The Foinavon Field is a new oilfield in the North Atlantic Ocean where the sea is much deeper.

Key

M4 S	Motorway, service area
	Motorway, junction
A31	Primary route
A475	Other main road
	Passenger railway
	County boundary
	National boundary
✈ ⊛	Airport / with Customs
	International ferry port
	Domestic ferry port
	City / Urban area
○	Town area
	River / Lake

	800m +
	600 - 800m
	400 - 600m
	200 - 400m
	75 - 200m
	0 - 75m

One millimetre on the map is the same as 2 kilometre on the ground

0   20   40   60   80

People all over the world have heard of the Loch Ness Monster. Loch Ness is one of the lochs in the Great Glen, a deep valley which divides the Scottish highlands.

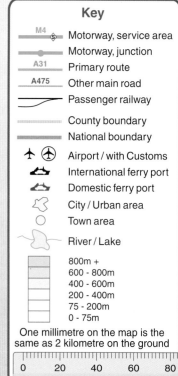

In the Past

The Romans built Hadrian's Wall to keep the Picts and Scots out. Angles and Vikings later settled in Scotland. The country was united in the ninth century under King Kenneth I. In 1296 Edward I of England claimed the Scottish throne but Robert the Bruce forced the English out. In 1603 King James VI of Scotland became King James I of England.

Largest Settlements

Glasgow	697 000
Edinburgh	438 000
Aberdeen	211 000
Dundee	175 000
Paisley	95 000

100 000 people

Scotland has the finest winter sports in the United Kingdom. Aviemore is the best known centre.

Shetland's Viking past is still celebrated today.

CENTRAL SCOTLAND

Most of Scotland's population lives in the lowland central area. The two great cities of Glasgow and Edinburgh are located here.

In 1750 Edinburgh was the second largest city in the British Isles. In the early nineteenth century Glasgow became Scotland's largest city. Glasgow's population grew to over one million in the 1950s.

Central Scotland was once a great engineering centre. Ships, railway engines and machinery were built and exported around the world. These industries have shrunk leading to large scale unemployment.

Edinburgh has always been a popular city for tourists. Its famous castle and arts festival attract visitors from all over the world.

Tourism and office jobs have increased in Glasgow, where modern offices have appeared next to the city's historic buildings.

New industry has been attracted to central Scotland. High technology linked to computers has produced new jobs in electronics.

WALES

Wales is a country of great contrasts. South Wales is very densely populated, especially in the valleys which lead down to Cardiff. In parts of central and North Wales the sheep outnumber the people. The Welsh mountains contain many rare plants. Tourists, especially climbers and walkers, are attracted to the rugged beauty of the land.

28

Key

M4 $_S$	Motorway, service area
	Motorway, junction
A31	Primary route
A475	Other main road
	Passenger railway
	County boundary
	National boundary
✈ ✈	Airport / with Customs
	International ferry port
	Domestic ferry port
	City / Urban area
○	Town area
	River / Lake

800m +
600 - 800m
400 - 600m
200 - 400m
75 - 200m
0 - 75m

One millimetre on the map is the same as 1 kilometre on the ground

0   10   20   30   40

In the Past

Different rulers of England tried to conquer Wales but always found the mountains a great problem. There the Welsh could avoid invaders and attack them when ready. In the Middle Ages the English kings built magnificent castles and towns into which they moved settlers in an attempt to control the Welsh.

Dim palmant am 800 llath No footway for 800yds

The Welsh language is strongest in North Wales but is growing in popularity in other parts of Wales. About 20% of people speak Welsh.

Largest Settlements

Cardiff   290 000
Swansea   172 000
Newport   111 000
Ebbw Vale   77 000
Merthyr Tydfil   57 000

100 000 people

Wales has been very successful in attracting Japanese companies to build factories. These have helped replace the jobs lost by the decline of industries such as coal, steel and slate.

NORTH WEST ENGLAND

Key

M4 ⓢ	Motorway, service area
	Motorway, junction
A31	Primary route
A475	Other main road
	Passenger railway
	County boundary
	National boundary
✈ ✈	Airport / with Customs
	International ferry port
	Domestic ferry port
	City / Urban area
○	Town area
	River / Lake

	800m +
	600 - 800m
	400 - 600m
	200 - 400m
	75 - 200m
	0 - 75m

One millimetre on the map is the same as 1 kilometre on the ground

0 10 20 30 40

North West England is a very varied region. The Pennines contain many towns which grew rapidly during the nineteenth century, their industry based on textiles. The Lake District is possibly England's most beautiful area. The south contains great cities like Manchester and Liverpool, famous for their industry, music and football.

Blackpool Pleasure Beach is the United Kingdom's most popular tourist attraction and Blackpool is the busiest seaside holiday resort. Rides like 'The Big One' attract millions of visitors.

Largest Settlements

Manchester	450 000
Liverpool	450 000
Salford	350 000
Stockport	292 000
Warrington	190 000

100 000 people

In the Past

The Romans built major towns like Chester and Manchester as well as forts all the way to Hadrian's Wall. Later most of the region became Saxon but Norwegian Vikings settled in the Lake District and near the coast. Large numbers of people from all over the British Isles and Europe set out for new lives in America from the port of Liverpool.

The Lake District has magnificent mountains, lakes and valleys. It is England's wettest area but remains very popular with visitors. It was home to many great poets.

NORTH EAST ENGLAND

York was an important city in Roman times and in the Viking period. The name York comes from the Danish name Jorvik. Today, York is an important tourist city, attracting people from all around the world.

Older industries were based on coal and iron which were mined in the region. Wool, from sheep in the hills, was turned into cloth in the towns east of the Pennines. In 1913 30% of the world's ships were built in the region, but today the industry has almost disappeared.

Largest Settlements

Leeds 529 000
Bradford 357 000
Newcastle 274 000
Kingston upon Hull 271 000
Sunderland 176 000

100 000 people

In the Past

The Romans built Hadrian's Wall which reached the North Sea near Newcastle upon Tyne. In Anglo-Saxon times the region was part of the Kingdom of Northumbria. Viking raiders found it easy to sail to this coast and Danish Vikings settled in large numbers. In the Middle Ages more abbeys and monasteries were built here than in any other region of Britain.

Most new jobs are in services. The Metro Centre near Gateshead attracts shoppers from long distances.

In Leeds, office jobs have increased. The first 'telephone bank' in Britain is based there.

MIDLANDS

Birmingham is the United Kingdom's second largest city. During the Industrial Revolution, Birmingham expanded rapidly. Unusually for a large city, it is not built on a river but it does have a network of canals.

Largest Settlements

Birmingham	1 000 000
Sheffield	528 000
Coventry	300 000
Leicester	280 000
Nottingham	280 000

1 million people
100 000 people

The car industry has been based in the region for many years. Rolls Royce, Jaguar and Land Rover, three of the world's best-known car names, are all based there.

In the Past

The Romans conquered the region and it became Romanised. Anglo-Saxons settled there after the Roman withdrawal. The region was part of the Kingdom of Mercia. King Offa of Mercia had a great ditch dug to mark the boundary between Mercia and Wales. It can still be walked along today. Later the region was attacked by Vikings and also by Welsh raiders who came from their hills, stole animals and goods, and returned. The world's first iron bridge was built at Ironbridge in 1778 – it crosses the River Severn.

The National Exhibition Centre (NEC) has been built at Birmingham, attracting international visitors to major events.

EAST MIDLANDS and EAST ANGLIA

The region is the flattest in the United Kingdom. Some of the land east of Peterborough is below sea level. It was marshland until the land was drained – now it is rich farm land. The town of Ely stands on high ground which was once an island.

In the west of the region are large cities and coalfields. Close to Nottingham is the remains of Sherwood Forest – the setting for the legendary adventures of Robin Hood and his merry men.

This helmet was part of the remains found in the burial ship at Sutton Hoo. King Radwald died in about AD625 and was buried in his ship beneath a huge mound of soil.

Key

M4 $\otimes$	Motorway, service area
A31	Motorway, junction
A31	Primary route
A475	Other main road
	Passenger railway
	County boundary
	National boundary
✈ ✈	Airport / with Customs
	International ferry port
	Domestic ferry port
	City / Urban area
○	Town area
	River / Lake

	800m +
	600 - 800m
	400 - 600m
	200 - 400m
	75 - 200m
	0 - 75m

One millimetre on the map is the same as 1 kilometre on the ground

0   10   20   30   40

Largest Settlements

Northampton	186 000	
Norwich	173 000	
Colchester	151 000	
Peterborough	136 000	
Ipswich	120 000	

100 000 people

In the Past

The Roman occupation of Britain was seriously threatened when Queen Boudicca led her tribe, the Iceni, against the Romans. The Roman colony at Colchester was destroyed before Boudicca was defeated. Following the departure of the Romans the region was conquered first by Anglo-Saxons and later by Danish Vikings.

East of Norwich are the Norfolk Broads – an area of lakes, rivers and channels. Tourists come here for boating holidays. It is also home to many rare birds, flowers, insects and plants.

Some of the world's best racehorses are trained in the Newmarket area.

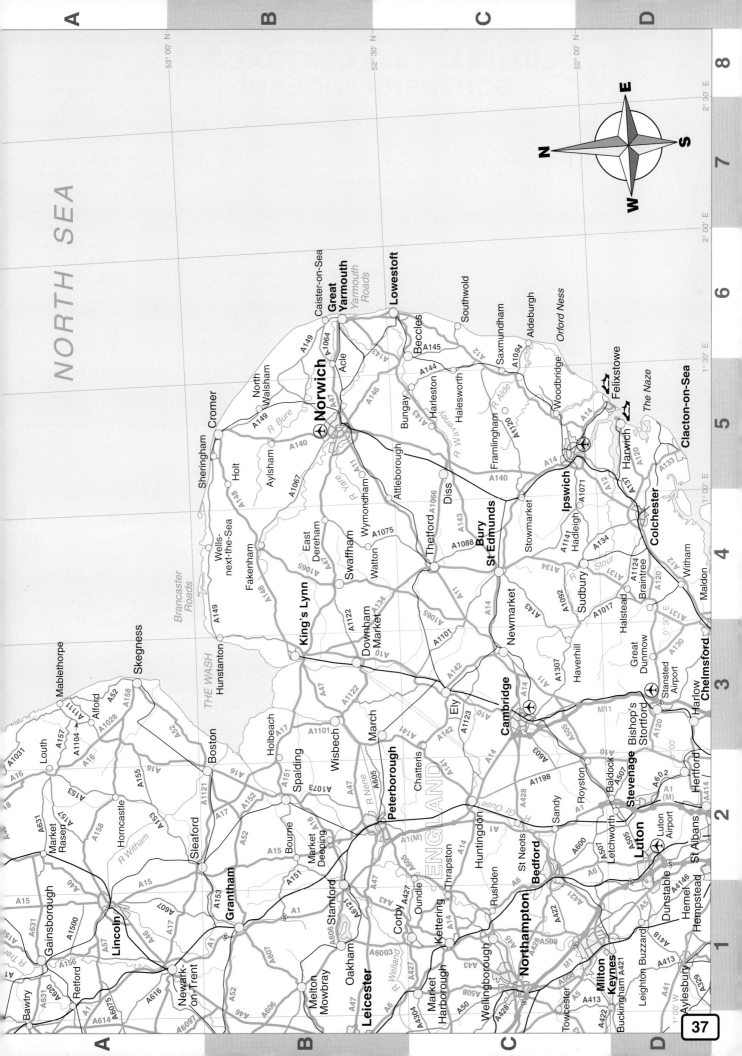

NORTH SEA

37

SOUTH EAST and CENTRAL SOUTHERN ENGLAND

London is the hub of this region. Motorways, roads and railways run out from London, like the spokes of a wheel, to the rest of the region. Every week millions of people travel into London to work, shop or visit.

London was once the world's largest city. Today it is an important world centre for trade, industry, banking, entertainment and tourism. Parts of old London such as the docklands have been demolished and replaced with modern office blocks and housing.

Key

M4 ⓈⓈ	Motorway, service area
●	Motorway, junction
A31	Primary route
A475	Other main road
	Passenger railway
	County boundary
	National boundary
✈ ⊕	Airport / with Customs
	International ferry port
	Domestic ferry port
	City / Urban area
○	Town area
	River / Lake

	800m +
	600 - 800m
	400 - 600m
	200 - 400m
	75 - 200m
	0 - 75m

One millimetre on the map is the same as 1 kilometre on the ground

0 10 20 30 40

Largest Settlements

London	7 650 000
Southampton	196 000
Milton Keynes	184 000
Portsmouth	181 000
Swindon	173 000

■ 1 million people
▮ 100 000 people

The airports of the South East include Heathrow, the world's busiest airport for international passengers.

In the Past

Invaders and settlers have entered the region from Continental Europe throughout history. Julius Caesar came briefly in 55BC, but a full Roman invasion had to wait until AD43. The Romans soon took control of the South East. They founded London, which became the capital of Roman Britain. In the fifth century, the region was invaded by Anglo-Saxons and Jutes. The rule of the Anglo-Saxons lasted until the Vikings conquered the South East. In 1066 William the Conqueror landed at Pevensey, near Hastings. This was the last successful invasion of England.

Felixstowe
Harwich
Sheerness
Tilbury
Ramsgate
Dover
Folkestone
Southampton
Portsmouth
Newhaven
Poole

The coast is dotted with ports both large and small. Southampton is important both for trade and cruise ships. The QE2 sails from there.

SOUTH WEST ENGLAND

South West England contains the beautiful countryside and villages of the Cotswolds, Salisbury Plain where Stonehenge stands and rich farmland around Gloucester and south of Bristol. The hills of the south give way to rugged, wild moorland further west. Dartmoor and Exmoor are both National Parks. They can be dangerous when the snow or mist set in.

Stonehenge is an immense stone circle built around 1500BC. Its exact purpose is unknown.

Largest Settlements

Bristol	370 000
Plymouth	242 000
Bournemouth	154 000
Exeter	103 000
Gloucester	97 000

100 000 people

In the Past

There is much evidence of the settlements of the Ancient Britons, like hill-top villages, standing stones, burial chambers and stone circles. The city of Bath was the Roman town Aquae Sulis. Parts of the Roman baths can still be visited today. Bristol, the largest city in the South West, developed on the rivers Severn and Avon. The city grew rich on trade in wool, wine, tobacco, chocolate and slaves. Cornwall remained different from most of England for many centuries. The Cornish language died out but Cornish place names and saints' names remain.

Bristol is another ancient dock city which has had to redevelop its docklands because of changes in trade and the size of ships.

The Atlantic Ocean brings warm sea and air to the South West. Tourists visit the region for the warm summers, sandy beaches and hills. Parts of the region are so busy in summer that towns have been closed to any more traffic.

NORTHERN IRELAND

Northern Ireland is a province of just over 1.5 million people. There are only two large settlements in the province, Belfast and Londonderry (Derry). Many people live in small settlements, particularly in the farming areas.

Violence between the Republicans and the Loyalists over many years means industries such as tourism have not developed as strongly as they might. Peace will provide a great economic boost to the area.

Key

M4 $	Motorway, service area
	Motorway, junction
A31	Primary route
A475	Other main road
	Passenger railway
	County boundary
	National boundary
✈ ✈	Airport / with Customs
	International ferry port
	Domestic ferry port
	City / Urban area
○	Town area
	River / Lake

	800m +
	600 - 800m
	400 - 600m
	200 - 400m
	75 - 200m
	0 - 75m

One millimetre on the map is the same as 1 kilometre on the ground

0   10   20   30   40

Belfast is the largest city in Northern Ireland, although its population has been falling. It was over 400,000 in 1971, but is now about 280,000. Belfast is an industrial city with a port. Shipbuilding and aircraft manufacture are still important industries in the city.

In the Past

What is now Northern Ireland has had several invasions. Both the Vikings and Normans invaded. The English ruled Ireland from the twelfth century, but rebellions were frequent. From the sixteenth century many settlers from England and Scotland moved to Ulster, the north-eastern part of Ireland. In 1921 Ireland was divided. Most of Ulster remained in the UK.

Largest Settlements

Belfast	279 000	
Londonderry/Derry	72 000	
Bangor	52 000	
Lisburn	42 000	
Ballymena	28 000	

100 000 people

Dairy farming is well-suited to the cool, wet climate.

One of Northern Ireland's most famous physical features is the Giant's Causeway. It was formed when volcanic lava broke through the earth's surface. This lava is called basalt. In the open air it began to cool and contracted (shrank) into polygons. From above it looks like a stone honeycomb.

UK IN EUROPE
People

As people grow older they need more care. If there are not enough young people who will care for the elderly?

Population
Four Largest European

Russia
150 million

Germany
82 million

UK
58 million

Italy
58 million

Four Smallest

Luxembourg
408,000

Iceland
270,000

Andorra
65,000

Liechtenstein
30,000

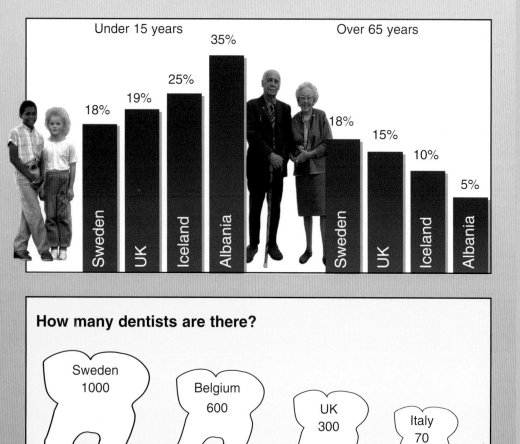

Under 15 years — Sweden 18%, UK 19%, Iceland 25%, Albania 35%

Over 65 years — Sweden 18%, UK 15%, Iceland 10%, Albania 5%

How many dentists are there?

Sweden 1000

Belgium 600

UK 300

Italy 70

Number of dentists for every million people

How do people die?

Cause of death		UK	France	Spain
H	Heart disease	50%	37%	50%
	Lung problems	11%	7%	10%
C	Cancer	24%	24%	18%
	Injuries	3%	8%	4%

R.I.P

UK IN EUROPE
Consumers

Norway 650

Denmark 1350

UK 1700

Austria 1900

Who smokes the most?

Poland 2650

Cigarettes smoked per person in a year

Greece 3250

Who likes potatoes?

143kg Poland

113kg UK

66kg Austria

42kg Italy

Potatoes eaten in kilos for each person per year

Anyone for tea?
Kilos of tea drunk per person per year

3.1kg Ireland

2.5kg UK

0.7kg Netherlands

0.1kg Belgium

In the home
% of homes

		France	UK	Norway	Finland
Television		98%	98%	99%	72%
Video		10%	61%	22%	5%
Dishwasher		28%	9%	24%	15%
Freezer		37%	39%	80%	52%

45

UK IN EUROPE
Production

How much of a country's glass is recycled?

Netherlands 62%

Switzerland 47%

France 26%

UK 13%

How much of the country's wealth comes from agriculture, industry and services?

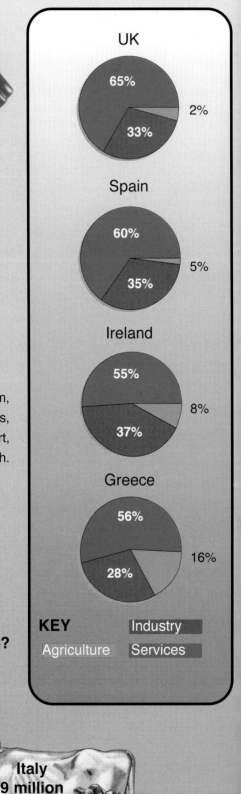

UK
65%
33%
2%

Spain
60%
35%
5%

Ireland
55%
37%
8%

Greece
56%
28%
16%

KEY
Industry
Agriculture
Services

Services include tourism, banking, shops, entertainment, transport, education and health.

How many cattle are there?

France 21 million

UK 12 million

Italy 9 million

Norway 1 million

Place	Country	Grid		Lat	Long
berdare	Wales	E2	29	51°43′N	3°27′W
berdeen	Scot	M6	25	57°09′N	2°08′W
berfeldy	Scot	J5	25	56°37′N	3°52′W
bergele	Wales	D5	29	53°17′N	3°35′W
bersoch	Wales	B4	29	52°50′N	4°30′W
berystwyth	Wales	C3	29	52°25′N	4°05′W
bingdon	Eng	B2	39	51°40′N	1°17′W
characle	Scot	E5	25	56°44′N	5°48′W
chnasheen	Scot	F7	25	57°35′N	5°04′W
irdrie	Scot	C5	27	55°52′N	3°59′W
ldeburgh	Eng	C6	37	52°09′N	1°36′E
lford	Scot	L6	25	57°14′N	2°42′W
lfreton	Eng	E5	35	53°06′N	1°23′W
lloa	Scot	B5	27	56°07′N	3°48′W
lnwick	Eng	A4	33	55°25′N	1°43′W
lston	Eng	F4	31	54°49′N	2°27′W
lton	Eng	C3	39	51°09′N	0°59′W
mbleside	Eng	E3	31	54°26′N	2°58′W
mersham	Eng	B3	39	51°41′N	0°36′W
mesbury	Eng	C1	39	51°10′N	1°47′W
mlwch	Wales	C5	29	53°25′N	4°20′W
ndover	Eng	C2	39	51°12′N	1°29′W
nnan	Eng	E6	27	54°59′N	3°15′W
ntrim	N Ire	B6	43	54°43′N	6°14′W
ppleby-in-Westmorland	Eng	F4	31	54°35′N	2°29′W
rbroath	Scot	A7	27	56°34′N	2°35′W
rdrossan	Scot	C3	27	55°39′N	4°48′W
rmagh	N Ire	C5	43	54°20′N	6°39′W
shbourne	Eng	D5	35	53°01′N	1°43′W
shby-de-la-Zouch	Eng	E4	35	52°45′N	1°28′W
shford	Eng	C6	39	51°09′N	0°52′E
shington	Eng	A4	33	55°11′N	1°34′W
shton-under-Lyne	Eng	C5	35	53°29′N	2°05′W
uchterarder	Scot	B5	27	56°18′N	3°42′W
viemore	Scot	J6	25	57°11′N	3°50′W
vonmouth	Eng	A7	41	51°30′N	2°41′W
ylesbury	Eng	B3	39	51°49′N	0°49′W
ylsham	Eng	B5	37	52°48′N	1°15′E
yr	Scot	D3	27	55°28′N	4°37′W
ala	Wales	D4	29	52°55′N	3°36′W
allachulish	Scot	F5	25	56°41′N	5°08′W
allater	Scot	K6	25	57°03′N	3°08′W
allycastle	N Ire	A6	43	55°12′N	6°15′W
allymena	N Ire	B6	43	54°50′N	6°16′W
anbridge	N Ire	C6	43	54°20′N	6°16′W
anbury	Eng	E3	35	52°04′N	1°20′W
anff	Scot	L7	25	57°40′N	2°32′W
angor	N Ire	B7	43	54°39′N	5°40′W
angor	Wales	C5	29	53°13′N	4°08′W
armouth	Wales	C4	29	52°43′N	4°03′W
arnard Castle	Eng	A3	33	54°33′N	1°55′W
arnsley	Eng	B1	33	53°33′N	1°29′W
arnstaple	Eng	B4	41	51°05′N	4°03′W
arrow-in-Furness	Eng	D3	31	54°07′N	3°14′W
asildon	Eng	B5	39	51°35′N	0°30′E
asingstoke	Eng	C2	39	51°16′N	1°05′W
ath	Eng	B8	41	51°23′N	2°22′W
athgate	Scot	C5	27	55°54′N	3°38′W
attle	Eng	D5	39	50°55′N	0°29′E
eaconsfield	Eng	B3	39	51°36′N	0°39′W
edford	Eng	C2	37	52°08′N	0°28′W
elfast	N Ire	B7	43	54°38′N	5°55′W
erwick-upon-Tweed	Eng	A5	33	55°46′N	2°00′W
etws-y-Coed	Wales	D5	29	53°05′N	3°48′W
exhill	Eng	D5	39	50°51′N	0°28′E
cester	Eng	B2	39	51°54′N	1°09′W
ggar	Scot	C5	27	55°37′N	3°31′W
rkenhead	Eng	D1	31	53°23′N	3°03′W
rmingham	Eng	D3	35	52°29′N	1°52′W
shop Auckland	Eng	A3	33	54°39′N	1°41′W
shop's Stortford	Eng	B5	39	51°52′N	0°10′E
ackburn	Eng	F2	31	53°45′N	2°29′W
ackpool	Eng	D2	31	53°49′N	3°02′W
yth	Eng	A4	33	55°08′N	1°31′W
ognor Regis	Eng	D3	39	50°47′N	0°40′W
olton	Eng	F2	31	53°34′N	2°26′W
onar Bridge	Scot	H7	25	57°53′N	4°20′W
ootle	Eng	D1	31	53°27′N	3°00′W
oston	Eng	B2	37	52°59′N	0°01′W
ourne	Eng	B2	37	52°46′N	0°23′W
ournemouth	Eng	D1	39	50°43′N	1°53′W
rackley	Eng	E3	35	52°02′N	1°09′W
racknell	Eng	C3	39	51°24′N	0°45′W
radford	Eng	A1	33	53°47′N	1°45′W
raemar	Scot	K6	25	57°00′N	3°25′W
rampton	Eng	E4	31	54°57′N	2°44′W
rechin	Scot	L5	25	56°44′N	2°39′W
recon	Wales	E2	29	51°57′N	3°23′W
rentwood	Eng	B5	39	51°37′N	0°19′E
ridgend	Wales	D2	29	51°31′N	3°35′W
ridgnorth	Eng	C5	35	52°32′N	2°25′W
ridgwater	Eng	B6	41	51°08′N	2°59′W
rigg	Eng	D1	33	53°33′N	0°29′W
righton	Eng	D5	39	50°50′N	0°08′W
ristol	Eng	B7	41	51°29′N	2°34′W
romsgrove	Eng	C3	35	52°20′N	2°04′W
rough	Eng	F4	31	54°31′N	2°19′W
Buckfastleigh	Eng	D5	41	50°29′N	3°47′W
Buckingham	Eng	F2	35	52°00′N	0°59′W
Bungay	Eng	C5	37	52°27′N	1°26′E
Burgess Hill	Eng	D4	39	50°58′N	0°08′W
Burnham-on-Crouch	Eng	B6	39	51°38′N	0°49′E
Burnley	Eng	F2	31	53°47′N	2°15′W
Burton upon Trent	Eng	D4	35	52°48′N	1°38′W
Bury	Eng	F2	31	53°35′N	2°18′W
Bury St Edmunds	Eng	C4	37	52°15′N	0°43′E
Buxton	Eng	D5	35	53°15′N	1°54′W
Caernarfon	Wales	C5	29	53°08′N	4°16′W
Caerphilly	Wales	E2	29	51°34′N	3°13′W
Callander	Scot	B4	27	56°14′N	4°12′W
Cambridge	Eng	C3	37	52°12′N	0°08′E
Camelford	Eng	C3	41	50°37′N	4°41′W
Campbeltown	Scot	D1	27	55°25′N	5°37′W
Cannich	Scot	G6	25	57°21′N	4°46′W
Canterbury	Eng	C7	39	51°16′N	1°04′E
Cardiff	Wales	E1	29	51°29′N	3°10′W
Cardigan	Wales	B3	29	52°05′N	4°40′W
Carlisle	Eng	E4	31	54°53′N	2°57′W
Carmarthen	Wales	C2	29	51°52′N	4°18′W
Carnoustie	Scot	A7	27	56°30′N	2°42′W
Carrickfergus	N Ire	B7	43	54°42′N	5°49′W
Castlebay	Scot	A5	25	56°57′N	7°29′W
Castleford	Eng	B1	33	53°43′N	1°21′W
Charlestown of Aberlour	Scot	K6	25	57°28′N	3°14′W
Chatham	Eng	C6	39	51°22′N	0°32′E
Cheddar	Eng	B7	41	51°17′N	2°47′W
Chelmsford	Eng	B5	39	51°44′N	0°28′E
Cheltenham	Eng	C2	35	51°54′N	2°05′W
Chepstow	Wales	F2	29	51°38′N	2°40′W
Chester	Eng	B5	35	53°11′N	2°53′W
Chester-le-Street	Eng	A3	33	54°51′N	1°34′W
Chesterfield	Eng	D5	35	53°14′N	1°25′W
Chichester	Eng	D3	39	50°50′N	0°46′W
Chorley	Eng	E2	31	53°39′N	2°38′W
Christchurch	Eng	D1	39	50°44′N	1°47′W
Cirencester	Eng	D2	35	51°43′N	1°58′W
Clacton-on-Sea	Eng	B7	39	51°48′N	1°09′E
Clitheroe	Eng	F3	31	53°52′N	2°23′W
Cockermouth	Eng	D4	31	54°40′N	3°21′W
Colchester	Eng	B6	39	51°53′N	0°54′E
Coldstream	Scot	A8	27	55°39′N	2°15′W
Coleraine	N Ire	A5	43	55°10′N	6°41′W
Colwyn Bay	Wales	D5	29	53°18′N	3°42′W
Consett	Eng	A3	33	54°51′N	1°51′W
Cookstown	N Ire	B5	43	54°38′N	6°45′W
Corby	Eng	C1	37	52°30′N	0°42′W
Coventry	Eng	D3	35	52°24′N	1°30′W
Cowes	Eng	D2	39	50°45′N	1°18′W
Crawley	Eng	C4	39	51°07′N	0°11′W
Crewe	Eng	C5	35	53°05′N	2°52′W
Crianlarich	Scot	B3	27	56°24′N	4°37′W
Crieff	Scot	B5	27	56°22′N	3°50′W
Cromarty	Scot	H7	25	57°41′N	4°02′W
Cromer	Eng	B5	37	52°56′N	1°18′E
Croydon	Eng	C4	39	51°22′N	0°05′W
Cumbernauld	Scot	C5	27	55°57′N	3°59′W
Cumnock	Scot	D3	27	55°27′N	4°15′W
Cwmbran	Wales	E2	29	51°39′N	3°01′W
Dagenham	Eng	B5	39	51°32′N	0°08′E
Dalbeattie	Scot	E5	27	54°56′N	3°49′W
Dalkeith	Scot	C6	27	55°54′N	3°03′W
Darlington	Eng	A3	33	54°31′N	1°34′W
Dartford	Eng	C5	39	51°26′N	0°12′E
Dartmouth	Eng	D5	41	50°21′N	3°34′W
Daventry	Eng	E3	35	52°15′N	1°09′W
Dawlish	Eng	C6	41	50°35′N	3°28′W
Deal	Eng	C7	39	51°13′N	1°24′E
Derby	Eng	D4	35	52°55′N	1°28′W
Devizes	Eng	C1	39	51°21′N	1°59′W
Dewsbury	Eng	A1	33	53°40′N	1°38′W
Dingwall	Scot	H7	25	57°35′N	4°25′W
Doncaster	Eng	B1	33	53°31′N	1°08′W
Dorchester	Eng	C8	41	50°43′N	2°27′W
Dorking	Eng	C4	39	51°14′N	0°20′W
Dover	Eng	C7	39	51°07′N	1°18′E
Driffield	Eng	D2	33	54°02′N	0°28′W
Drynoch	Scot	D6	25	57°18′N	6°18′W
Dudley	Eng	C4	35	52°31′N	2°06′W
Dufftown	Scot	K6	25	57°26′N	3°07′W
Dumbarton	Scot	C3	27	55°57′N	4°33′W
Dumfries	Scot	D5	27	55°04′N	3°36′W
Dunbar	Scot	C7	27	56°00′N	2°31′W
Dundee	Scot	B7	27	56°29′N	3°02′W
Dunfermline	Scot	B6	27	56°04′N	3°26′W
Dungannon	N Ire	C5	43	54°29′N	6°46′W
Duns	Scot	C8	27	55°46′N	2°21′W
Dunstable	Eng	B3	39	51°53′N	0°32′W
Durham	Eng	A3	33	54°47′N	1°34′W
Durness	Scot	G9	25	58°34′N	4°45′W
East Grinstead	Eng	C4	39	51°08′N	0°01′W
East Kilbride	Scot	C4	27	56°02′N	4°42′W
Eastbourne	Eng	D5	39	50°47′N	0°16′E
Eastleigh	Eng	D2	39	50°58′N	1°21′W
Ebbw Vale	Wales	E2	29	51°44′N	3°11′W
Edinburgh	Scot	C6	27	55°57′N	3°10′W
Elgin	Scot	K7	25	57°39′N	3°19′W
Ellesmere	Eng	B4	35	53°16′N	2°53′W
Ellon	Scot	M6	25	57°22′N	2°04′W
Ely	Eng	C3	37	52°24′N	0°16′E
Enniskillen	N Ire	C3	43	54°20′N	7°34′W
Esher	Eng	C4	39	51°22′N	0°21′W
Evesham	Eng	D3	35	52°05′N	1°57′W
Exeter	Eng	C5	41	50°43′N	3°31′W
Exmouth	Eng	C6	41	50°37′N	3°24′W
Fakenham	Eng	B4	37	52°50′N	0°51′E
Falkirk	Scot	C5	27	56°00′N	3°47′W
Falmouth	Eng	D2	41	50°09′N	5°04′W
Felixstowe	Eng	B7	37	51°58′N	1°21′E
Ffestiniog	Wales	D4	29	52°57′N	3°56′W
Fishguard	Wales	B2	29	52°00′N	4°59′W
Fleetwood	Eng	D2	31	53°55′N	3°02′W
Folkestone	Eng	C7	39	51°05′N	1°10′E
Forfar	Scot	L5	25	56°39′N	2°53′W
Formby	Eng	D2	31	53°33′N	3°04′W
Fort Augustus	Scot	G6	25	57°09′N	4°41′W
Fort William	Scot	F5	25	56°49′N	5°06′W
Fortuneswell	Eng	C8	41	50°34′N	2°27′W
Frome	Eng	B8	41	51°13′N	2°19′W
Gainsborough	Eng	A1	37	53°24′N	0°46′W
Gairloch	Scot	E7	25	57°43′N	5°41′W
Galashiels	Scot	C7	27	55°37′N	2°48′W
Gateshead	Eng	A3	33	54°56′N	1°37′W
Glasgow	Scot	C4	27	55°52′N	4°15′W
Glastonbury	Eng	B7	41	51°09′N	2°42′W
Glenrothes	Scot	A6	27	56°12′N	3°10′W
Gloucester	Eng	C2	35	51°52′N	2°14′W
Goole	Eng	C1	33	53°42′N	0°52′W
Gosport	Eng	D2	39	50°48′N	1°09′W
Grantham	Eng	B1	37	52°55′N	0°38′W
Gravesend	Eng	C5	39	51°27′N	0°23′E
Great Malvern	Eng	C3	35	52°07′N	2°19′W
Great Yarmouth	Eng	B6	37	52°36′N	1°44′E
Greenock	Scot	C3	27	55°57′N	4°46′W
Gretna	Scot	E6	27	55°00′N	3°04′W
Grimsby	Eng	D1	33	53°34′N	0°04′W
Guildford	Eng	C3	39	51°14′N	0°34′W
Guisborough	Eng	B3	33	54°32′N	1°05′W
Hailsham	Eng	D5	39	50°52′N	0°16′E
Halifax	Eng	A1	33	53°43′N	1°51′W
Hamilton	Scot	C4	27	55°46′N	4°02′W
Harlech	Wales	C4	29	52°52′N	4°06′W
Harrogate	Eng	A1	33	54°00′N	1°32′W
Hartlepool	Eng	B3	33	54°41′N	1°13′W
Harwich	Eng	B7	39	51°56′N	1°16′E
Hastings	Eng	D6	39	50°55′N	0°29′E
Hatfield	Eng	B4	39	51°45′N	0°14′W
Havant	Eng	D3	39	50°51′N	0°59′W
Haverhill	Eng	C3	37	52°05′N	0°26′E
Hawick	Scot	D7	27	55°26′N	2°47′W
Haywards Heath	Eng	C4	39	51°00′N	0°06′W
Heathfield	Eng	D5	39	50°58′N	0°15′E
Helmsdale	Scot	J8	25	58°07′N	3°39′W
Hemel Hempstead	Eng	B4	39	51°45′N	0°27′W
Henley-on-Thames	Eng	B3	39	51°32′N	0°54′W
Hereford	Eng	B3	35	52°04′N	2°42′W
Hertford	Eng	B4	39	51°48′N	0°05′W
Hexham	Eng	F4	31	54°58′N	2°06′W
Heysham	Eng	E3	31	54°03′N	2°54′W
High Wycombe	Eng	B3	39	51°38′N	0°45′W
Holyhead	Wales	B5	29	53°21′N	4°36′W
Honiton	Eng	C6	41	50°48′N	3°11′W
Horsham	Eng	C4	39	51°04′N	0°19′W
Howden	Eng	C1	33	53°45′N	0°52′W
Huddersfield	Eng	A1	33	53°39′N	1°47′W
Hungerford	Eng	C1	39	51°25′N	1°31′W
Hunstanton	Eng	B3	37	52°56′N	0°29′E
Huntingdon	Eng	C2	37	52°20′N	0°10′W
Hythe	Eng	C7	39	51°04′N	1°05′E
Ilford	Eng	B5	39	51°33′N	0°05′E
Ilkley	Eng	A1	33	53°55′N	1°49′W
Ilminster	Eng	C7	41	50°55′N	2°54′W
Immingham	Eng	D1	33	53°37′N	0°13′W
Inverarey	Scot	B2	27	56°14′N	5°04′W
Invergarry	Scot	G6	25	57°04′N	4°48′W
Invermoriston	Scot	G6	25	57°13′N	4°37′W
Inverness	Scot	H6	25	57°29′N	4°14′W
Ipswich	Eng	C5	37	52°03′N	1°09′E
Irvine	Scot	C3	27	55°37′N	4°40′W
Jedburgh	Scot	D7	27	55°29′N	2°33′W
John o' Groats	Scot	K9	25	58°38′N	3°04′W
Keith	Scot	L7	25	57°32′N	2°58′W
Kelso	Scot	C8	27	55°36′N	2°26′W
Kendal	Eng	E3	31	54°19′N	2°45′W
Keswick	Eng	D4	31	54°36′N	3°08′W
Kettering	Eng	C1	37	52°24′N	0°43′W
Kidderminster	Eng	C3	35	52°23′N	2°13′W

Place	Country	Grid	No.	Lat	Long
Killin	Scot	B4	27	56°28′N	4°19′W
Kilmarnock	Scot	C4	27	55°36′N	4°30′W
King's Lynn	Eng	B3	37	52°45′N	0°24′E
Kingsbridge	Eng	D5	41	50°17′N	3°47′W
Kingston upon Hull	Eng	D1	33	53°45′N	0°20′W
Kinlochewe	Scot	F7	25	57°36′N	5°18′W
Kinross	Scot	B6	27	56°12′N	3°26′W
Kintore	Scot	M6	25	57°14′N	2°21′W
Kirkcudbright	Scot	H1	25	54°50′N	4°03′W
Kirkwall	Scot	L9	25	58°59′N	2°57′W
Knaresborough	Eng	B2	33	54°01′N	1°27′W
Kyle of Lochalsh	Scot	E6	25	57°17′N	5°42′W
Lairg	Scot	H8	25	58°01′N	4°24′W
Lampeter	Wales	C3	29	52°07′N	4°05′W
Lanark	Scot	C5	27	55°40′N	3°46′W
Lancaster	Eng	E3	31	54°03′N	2°48′W
Larne	N Ire	B7	43	54°48′N	5°50′W
Lauder	Scot	C7	27	55°43′N	2°45′W
Leatherhead	Eng	C4	39	51°18′N	0°20′W
Ledmore	Scot	G8	25	58°04′N	4°58′W
Leeds	Eng	A1	33	53°48′N	1°32′W
Leicester	Eng	E4	35	52°38′N	1°08′W
Leighton Buzzard	Eng	B3	37	51°55′N	0°39′W
Leominster	Eng	B3	35	52°14′N	2°44′W
Lerwick	Scot	N9	25	60°09′N	1°09′W
Letchworth	Eng	B4	39	51°59′N	0°14′W
Leyburn	Eng	A2	33	54°19′N	1°49′W
Leyland	Eng	E2	31	53°42′N	2°41′W
Lincoln	Eng	A1	37	53°14′N	0°32′W
Lisburn	N Ire	C6	43	54°28′N	6°02′W
Littlehampton	Eng	D3	39	50°49′N	0°33′W
Liverpool	Eng	E1	31	53°25′N	2°56′W
Livingston	Scot	C5	27	55°54′N	3°30′W
Lizard	Eng	E2	41	49°58′N	5°12′W
Llandeilo	Wales	D2	29	51°53′N	3°59′W
Llandrindod Wells	Wales	E3	29	52°15′N	3°23′W
Llandudno	Wales	D5	29	53°19′N	3°49′W
Llanelli	Wales	C2	29	51°41′N	4°10′W
Llangollen	Wales	E4	29	52°58′N	3°10′W
Llanidloes	Wales	D3	29	52°27′N	3°32′W
Lochearnhead	Scot	B4	27	56°23′N	4°17′W
Lochgilphead	Scot	B2	27	56°02′N	5°26′W
Lochinver	Scot	F8	25	57°38′N	5°22′W
Lockerbie	Scot	D6	27	55°07′N	3°21′W
London	Eng	B4	39	51°31′N	0°06′W
Londonderry	N Ire	B4	43	54°59′N	7°20′W
Longtown	Eng	E5	31	55°00′N	2°58′W
Lossiemouth	Scot	K7	25	57°43′N	3°17′W
Loughborough	Eng	E4	35	52°46′N	1°12′W
Lowestoft	Eng	C6	37	52°28′N	1°44′E
Ludlow	Eng	B3	35	52°22′N	2°43′W
Lurgan	N Ire	C6	43	54°27′N	6°20′W
Luton	Eng	B4	39	51°53′N	0°25′W
Lydd	Eng	D6	39	50°57′N	0°55′E
Lyme Regis	Eng	C7	41	50°44′N	2°56′W
Lytham St Anne's	Eng	D2	31	53°44′N	3°00′W
Mablethorpe	Eng	A3	37	53°21′N	0°16′E
Macclesfield	Eng	C5	35	53°15′N	2°08′W
Maidenhead	Eng	B3	39	51°31′N	0°44′W
Maidstone	Eng	C5	39	51°16′N	0°32′E
Maldon	Eng	B6	39	51°44′N	0°40′E
Mallaig	Scot	E5	25	57°00′N	5°50′W
Manchester	Eng	F1	31	53°29′N	2°15′W
Mansfield	Eng	E5	35	53°09′N	1°12′W
Margate	Eng	C7	39	51°23′N	1°23′E
Market Drayton	Eng	C4	35	52°54′N	2°29′W
Market Harborough	Eng	C1	37	52°29′N	0°55′W
Marlborough	Eng	C1	39	51°25′N	1°44′W
Matlock	Eng	D5	35	53°08′N	1°34′W
Melrose	Scot	C7	27	55°36′N	2°43′W
Melton Mowbray	Eng	B1	37	52°46′N	0°53′W
Menai Bridge	Wales	C5	29	53°14′N	4°10′W
Merthyr Tydfil	Wales	E2	29	51°45′N	3°22′W
Middlesbrough	Eng	B3	33	54°33′N	1°12′W
Midhurst	Eng	D3	39	50°59′N	0°44′W
Milford Haven	Wales	A2	29	51°42′N	5°04′W
Milton Keynes	Eng	C1	37	52°02′N	0°45′W
Minehead	Eng	B6	41	51°12′N	3°29′W
Moffat	Scot	D6	27	55°20′N	3°27′W
Mold	Wales	E5	29	53°10′N	3°09′W
Monmouth	Wales	F2	29	51°48′N	2°43′W
Montrose	Scot	M5	25	56°42′N	2°28′W
Morecambe	Eng	E3	31	54°04′N	2°52′W
Morpeth	Eng	A4	33	55°10′N	1°41′W
Motherwell	Scot	C5	27	55°47′N	3°59′W
Nairn	Scot	J7	25	57°35′N	3°52′W
Nantwich	Eng	B5	35	53°04′N	2°31′W
Neath	Wales	D2	29	51°40′N	5°02′W
New Galloway	Scot	D4	27	55°04′N	4°08′W
Newark-on-Trent	Eng	A1	37	53°04′N	0°49′W
Newbury	Eng	C2	39	51°24′N	1°19′W
Newcastle	N Ire	C7	43	54°13′N	5°55′W
Newcastle upon Tyne	Eng	A3	33	54°58′N	1°36′W
Newcastle-under-Lyme	Eng	C5	35	53°01′N	2°13′W
Newhaven	Eng	D5	39	50°48′N	0°03′E
Newmarket	Eng	C3	37	52°15′N	0°24′E
Newport	Wales	F2	29	51°35′N	2°59′W
Newquay	Eng	D2	41	50°25′N	5°05′W
Newry	N Ire	C6	43	54°12′N	6°20′W
Newton Abbot	Eng	C5	41	50°32′N	3°36′W
Newton Aycliffe	Eng	A3	33	54°37′N	1°34′W
Newton Stewart	Scot	E4	27	54°57′N	4°29′W
Newtonards	N Ire	B7	43	54°36′N	5°41′W
Newtown	Wales	E4	29	52°31′N	3°18′W
North Berwick	Scot	B7	27	56°04′N	2°43′W
Northallerton	Eng	B2	33	54°21′N	1°25′W
Northampton	Eng	C1	37	52°15′N	0°54′W
Norwich	Eng	B5	37	52°38′N	1°18′E
Nottingham	Eng	E4	35	52°58′N	1°10′W
Nuneaton	Eng	D4	35	52°31′N	1°28′W
Oban	Scot	B2	27	56°25′N	5°28′W
Okehampton	Eng	C4	41	50°44′N	4°00′W
Oldham	Eng	F2	31	53°32′N	2°07′W
Omagh	N Ire	B4	43	54°35′N	7°20′W
Orpington	Eng	C4	39	51°22′N	0°05′E
Oswestry	Eng	A4	35	52°51′N	3°03′W
Oundle	Eng	C2	37	52°29′N	0°29′W
Oxford	Eng	B2	39	51°45′N	1°15′W
Paignton	Eng	D5	41	50°26′N	3°33′W
Paisley	Scot	C4	27	55°50′N	4°02′W
Peebles	Scot	C6	27	55°39′N	3°11′W
Pembroke	Wales	B2	29	51°40′N	4°55′W
Penarth	Wales	E1	29	51°26′N	3°10′W
Penrith	Eng	E4	31	54°40′N	2°45′W
Penzance	Eng	D1	41	50°07′N	5°33′W
Perth	Scot	B6	27	56°24′N	3°36′W
Peterborough	Eng	B2	37	52°35′N	0°14′W
Peterhead	Scot	N7	25	57°30′N	1°46′W
Pickering	Eng	C2	33	54°15′N	0°47′W
Pitlochry	Eng	J5	25	56°42′N	3°43′W
Plymouth	Eng	D4	41	50°23′N	4°09′W
Pontefract	Eng	B1	33	53°41′N	1°19′W
Pontypool	Wales	E2	29	51°42′N	3°02′W
Pontypridd	Wales	E2	29	51°36′N	3°20′W
Poole	Eng	C9	41	50°43′N	1°59′W
Port Askaig	Scot	D3	25	55°51′N	6°06′W
Port Talbot	Wales	D2	29	51°35′N	3°48′W
Portadown	N Ire	C6	43	54°25′N	6°28′W
Porthcawl	Eng	D1	29	51°29′N	3°42′W
Porthmadog	Wales	C4	29	52°55′N	4°08′W
Portpatrick	Scot	F1	25	54°51′N	5°07′W
Portsmouth	Eng	D2	39	50°48′N	1°04′W
Preston	Eng	E2	31	53°46′N	2°42′W
Prestwick	Scot	D3	27	55°30′N	4°37′W
Queensferry	Wales	E5	29	53°12′N	3°02′W
Ramsgate	Eng	C7	39	51°20′N	1°25′E
Reading	Eng	C3	39	51°27′N	0°58′W
Redcar	Eng	B3	33	54°37′N	1°03′W
Redruth	Eng	D2	41	50°14′N	5°14′W
Retford	Eng	A1	37	53°50′N	0°55′W
Rhondda	Wales	E2	29	51°39′N	3°29′W
Rhyl	Wales	E5	29	53°19′N	3°29′W
Richmond	Eng	C4	39	51°27′N	0°18′W
Richmond	Eng	A2	33	54°24′N	1°44′W
Ripon	Eng	A2	33	54°08′N	1°31′W
Rochdale	Eng	F2	31	53°37′N	2°10′W
Rochester	Eng	C6	39	51°23′N	0°29′E
Ross-on-Wye	Eng	B2	35	51°55′N	2°34′W
Rotherham	Eng	E5	35	53°26′N	1°21′W
Rothesay	Scot	C2	27	55°50′N	5°03′W
Royal Leamington Spa	Eng	D3	35	52°17′N	1°32′W
Royal Tunbridge Wells	Eng	C5	39	51°08′N	0°16′E
Rugby	Eng	E3	35	52°22′N	1°15′W
Runcorn	Eng	B5	35	53°20′N	2°43′W
Rushden	Eng	C1	37	52°17′N	0°36′W
Rye	Eng	D6	39	50°57′N	0°44′E
St Albans	Eng	B4	39	51°45′N	0°20′W
St Andrews	Scot	B7	27	56°20′N	2°47′W
St Austell	Eng	D3	41	50°20′N	4°47′W
St David's	Wales	A2	29	51°53′N	5°16′W
St Helens	Eng	E1	31	53°27′N	2°45′W
St Ives	Eng	D2	41	50°13′N	5°29′W
Salcombe	Eng	D5	41	50°14′N	3°46′W
Salford	Eng	F1	31	53°29′N	2°18′W
Salisbury	Eng	C1	39	51°04′N	1°48′W
Sandwich	Eng	C7	39	51°17′N	1°21′E
Sanquhar	Scot	D5	27	55°22′N	3°55′W
Scalasaig	Scot	D4	25	56°04′N	6°11′W
Scarborough	Eng	D2	33	54°17′N	0°25′W
Scunthorpe	Eng	C1	33	53°35′N	0°39′W
Seaham	Eng	B3	33	54°50′N	1°21′W
Seaton	Eng	C6	41	50°42′N	3°04′W
Sedbergh	Eng	F3	31	54°20′N	2°31′W
Selby	Eng	B1	33	53°47′N	1°04′W
Selkirk	Scot	C7	27	55°33′N	2°50′W
Settle	Eng	F3	31	54°04′N	2°17′W
Sevenoaks	Eng	C5	39	51°17′N	0°11′E
Shaftesbury	Eng	C8	41	51°00′N	2°12′W
Sheffield	Eng	D5	35	53°23′N	1°28′W
Sherborne	Eng	C7	41	50°57′N	2°31′W
Sheringham	Eng	B5	37	52°57′N	1°12′E
Shrewsbury	Eng	B4	35	52°42′N	2°45′W
Sidmouth	Eng	C6	41	50°41′N	3°14′W
Skegness	Eng	A3	37	53°09′N	0°20′E
Skipton	Eng	A1	33	53°57′N	2°01′W
Sleaford	Eng	B2	37	52°59′N	0°25′W
Slough	Eng	B3	39	51°30′N	0°34′W
South Shields	Eng	B3	33	54°05′N	1°26′W
Southampton	Eng	D2	39	50°55′N	1°24′W
Southend-on-Sea	Eng	B6	39	51°33′N	0°42′E
Southport	Eng	D2	31	53°39′N	2°59′W
Spalding	Eng	B2	37	52°47′N	0°09′W
Stafford	Eng	C4	35	52°48′N	2°07′W
Staines	Eng	C4	39	51°26′N	0°30′W
Stevenage	Eng	B4	39	51°54′N	0°11′W
Stirling	Scot	B5	27	56°07′N	3°56′W
Stockport	Eng	C5	35	53°25′N	2°09′W
Stockton-on-Tees	Eng	B3	33	54°35′N	1°20′W
Stoke-on-Trent	Eng	C5	35	53°01′N	2°11′W
Stonehaven	Scot	M5	25	56°58′N	2°12′W
Stornoway	Scot	D8	25	58°12′N	6°23′W
Stourbridge	Eng	C3	35	52°27′N	2°10′W
Strabane	N Ire	B4	43	54°49′N	7°28′W
Stranraer	Scot	E2	27	54°54′N	5°02′W
Stratford-upon-Avon	Eng	D3	35	52°12′N	1°43′W
Stroud	Eng	C2	35	51°45′N	2°13′W
Sudbury	Eng	C4	37	52°02′N	0°44′E
Sunderland	Eng	B3	33	54°55′N	1°23′W
Sutton	Eng	C4	39	51°22′N	0°12′W
Swanage	Eng	D1	39	50°36′N	1°58′W
Swansea	Wales	D2	29	51°38′N	3°57′W
Swindon	Eng	B1	39	51°34′N	1°46′W
Tadcaster	Eng	B1	33	53°53′N	1°16′W
Tamworth	Eng	D4	35	52°38′N	1°40′W
Taunton	Eng	B6	41	51°01′N	3°05′W
Tavistock	Eng	C4	41	50°33′N	4°08′W
Telford	Eng	C4	35	52°41′N	2°28′W
Thame	Eng	B3	39	51°45′N	0°59′W
Thetford	Eng	C4	37	52°25′N	0°45′E
Thirsk	Eng	B2	33	54°14′N	1°21′W
Thurso	Scot	J9	25	58°36′N	3°31′W
Tilbury	Eng	C5	39	51°28′N	0°22′E
Tobermory	Scot	D5	25	56°37′N	6°04′W
Tonbridge	Eng	C5	39	51°12′N	0°17′E
Tongue	Scot	H8	25	58°28′N	4°25′W
Torbay	Eng	D5	41	50°26′N	3°33′W
Torquay	Eng	D6	41	50°28′N	3°32′W
Towcester	Eng	C1	37	52°08′N	0°59′W
Troon	Scot	C3	27	55°32′N	4°39′W
Trowbridge	Eng	B8	41	51°19′N	2°12′W
Truro	Eng	D2	41	50°16′N	5°03′W
Tynemouth	Eng	B4	33	55°01′N	1°27′W
Ullapool	Scot	F7	25	57°54′N	5°10′W
Usk	Wales	F2	29	51°42′N	2°54′W
Uttoxeter	Eng	D4	35	52°54′N	1°52′W
Wakefield	Eng	B1	33	53°41′N	1°30′W
Walsall	Eng	D4	35	52°35′N	1°59′W
Warminster	Eng	B8	41	51°12′N	2°11′W
Warrington	Eng	B5	35	53°23′N	2°36′W
Warwick	Eng	D3	35	52°17′N	1°35′W
Watford	Eng	B4	39	51°40′N	0°24′W
Wellingborough	Eng	C1	37	52°18′N	0°41′W
Wellington	Eng	C6	41	50°59′N	3°13′W
Wells	Eng	B7	41	51°12′N	2°39′W
Welshpool	Wales	E4	29	52°39′N	3°09′W
Weston-super-Mare	Eng	B7	41	51°21′N	2°58′W
Wetherby	Eng	B1	33	53°56′N	1°23′W
Weymouth	Eng	C8	41	50°37′N	2°28′W
Whitby	Eng	C2	33	54°29′N	0°37′W
Whitchurch	Eng	B4	35	52°58′N	2°41′W
Whitehaven	Eng	C4	31	54°33′N	3°35′W
Whitstable	Eng	C7	39	51°21′N	1°02′E
Wick	Scot	K8	25	58°26′N	3°05′W
Wigan	Eng	E2	31	53°33′N	2°38′W
Wigtown	Scot	H1	25	54°52′N	4°26′W
Wilton	Eng	C1	39	51°05′N	1°52′W
Wincanton	Eng	B8	41	51°03′N	2°24′W
Winchester	Eng	C2	39	51°04′N	1°18′W
Windermere	Eng	E3	31	54°23′N	2°54′W
Withernsea	Eng	E1	33	53°44′N	0°02′W
Witney	Eng	B2	39	51°47′N	1°29′W
Woking	Eng	C3	39	51°19′N	0°33′W
Wolverhampton	Eng	C4	35	52°35′N	2°08′W
Wooler	Eng	A5	33	55°33′N	2°01′W
Worcester	Eng	C3	35	52°12′N	2°13′W
Workington	Eng	C4	31	54°38′N	3°33′W
Worthing	Eng	D3	39	50°49′N	0°23′W
Wrexham	Wales	F5	29	53°03′N	3°00′W
Wymondham	Eng	B5	37	52°34′N	1°07′E
Yarmouth	Eng	D2	39	50°42′N	1°30′W
Yeovil	Eng	C7	41	50°57′N	2°38′W
York	Eng	B1	33	53°57′N	1°06′W